THE WELL AT WINT

ELEANOR REES

The Well at Winter Solstice

with an afterword by Rosi Braidotti

SALT

CROMER

PUBLISHED BY SALT PUBLISHING 2019

2 4 6 8 10 9 7 5 3 1

Copyright © Eleanor Rees 2019

First published in Great Britain in 2019 by
Salt Publishing Ltd
12 Norwich Road, Cromer, Norfolk NR27 0AX United Kingdom

www.saltpublishing.com

Salt Publishing Limited Reg. No. 5293401

A CIP catalogue record for this book is available from the British Library

ISBN 978 1 78463 184 0 (Paperback edition)

Typeset in Sabon by Salt Publishing

Printed and bound in Great Britain by Clays Ltd, Elcograf S.p.A

Contents

'The void is a spectral realm; not even nothing can be free of ghosts.'

—KAREN BARAD

'The aim is to track the multiple, grounded and hence specific and diversified ways in which we are becoming knowing subjects, as 'otherwise other' than the dialectical oppositions and pejorative differences posited by classical humanist 'Man', and the supremacist assertions of "Anthropos".'

—ROSI BRAIDOTTI

'I have been in a multitude of shapes,
Before I assumed a consistent form.'

—TALIESIN

THE WELL AT WINTER SOLSTICE

St Seiriol's Well

A half-dressed man is sitting on the ledge
in a small hut, mortar-clad and damp with dew,
his knees folded to his chest, long hair as white
as the light which floods the grass;
each stalk bright like a lightning-struck tree.

And he is waiting for me to come and look
but I am still staring over the wall.
He has huge silver eyes like pools.
He is the pool, now a man
sat waiting to hold me,
to put his wet fingers around my waist

and I want to go to him
but I am also in the stream,
in the small brook which feeds the sea.

I am bare-foot and wearing only white
and the night is brittle cold and there is no-one else
apart from the moon
that glistens as I glisten

for I am the moon.
I am the reflection on the water as it runs,
sequential, down towards the sea.

I am a ripple, I am a wave
moving out into the sticky blue,
flattening and thinning – diffusing
like light, mixing with the swell
to form a deep swollen shadow;

and he is throwing copper pennies into the well,
which cascades waves like feathers over skin.

And he is walking to the stile
and the white limestone walls
and then he is not there at all,
never has been and I am now reeling,
coiling, the moon above is who I am
trickling down to the sea, to the sea.

Cool, crystal light within each gesture.
Clean and clear is my thought.
Crisp and horizontal is my action.

Two silver ovals shimmer back from my surfaces.
I thin outwards into the water

fully-lost and fully-formed.

Dawn

And I am a fish in the pond low near the rushes.
And I am in the branches of the trees in the high bird song.
And I am in the church tower leaning on the bell.
And I am in the grass as the trowel rips through.
And I am in the water as it strains through earth to the sea.
And I am in the thin heat of the April sun.

And he has gone in the daylight
back into the stone,
a body laid into the limestone dusted with moss.
He faces into the stone and watches the dark.

For he only shines when the moon
is full, for he is the moon,
the moon in the rock,
a fallen moon
rolling out from the source
and into the night,

a grounded moon,
a dry-landed moon

lying on the shore like an upturned ship.

DUSK

Psalms seep out from the priory like a whisper
as monks slice mackerel on wooden plates and hear
only the waves, the only constant, that rock
and hold them through the dark-filled night
and Seiriol in his sheepskin turns away from
the wind but speaks slowly to the trees
that swing and sing a soft harmony as birds
scratch their busy tunes into the sky;
and a woman in a purple raincoat
walks towards the well, a yellow ribbon
stained red dangles on the brambles
as the spring jangles its journey over rocks and away
and the woman reaches her pale fingers into the water,
swirls it around, puts the liquid to her lips,
slight-salt, iron-tang, and disappears
like vapour, like a splinter
and down into the rock like an axe
and down into the sea like a fish
and down into the soil like embers in a fire pit
where the bones of a lamb burn bright
and down, holding the lamb in her arms,
and down and out together, past the quarry, past the graveyard,
and the lamb has a child's face then a lamb's face
as they all unravel like the threads in her jumper
tumbling under and down, down into the earth.

Queen Fisher

I squawk at the sun's rest over the avenues,
        my children gone, rowed off in a small boat
                sunk at dawn,
            unborn in yolk,
                un-brewed they cluster in cries
        carried like rats in my beak
            as I fly fully-fledged
                along the shore of the river,
        openly raging,
            bare-breasted, alive;
    my crest lilts as I peck in the silt
            for my babies
                burrowed under, fully drowned, always fed.

They bleed into mud in the clutches of crabs;
        un-fleshed down rots as the salt rides in,
            and I raise my talons towards
                        the scarlet-sodden sunset
        and caw at the dry lands,
            the muscle-bound height of the landmass
                which leads to the woods
            where my nestlings should soar on the wind
                but there is no bright sound;
            no beat on the air, no current or pulse,
    just mud banks, old terns, a rusting bike,
                a ferry boat like a seal's muzzle
            in fresh water where salmon spawn.

I laid my eggs in the nest of the city.
It ate them for protein.

I fly at dusk,
      beaked head razor sharp,
            desire dead.

Salt Water

The river's mouth is sewn up
to stop its ebb and tide, its perpetual pull,

bone dry, thick dry, rough dry –

no more watery reach
beyond the horizon and our days.

I am a mouth wide open
sucking up the city's sounds:

I need words to wash our wounds.

Every chant, every incantation
is a sod of soil, a heavy weight,

ingested into acid
into blood and marrow

until my stomach turns,
mouths up a fresh spring morning

as the days rough over my tongue.
I lick my lips. I laugh.

I try to catch the words as they run
liquid into the clotting river,

a rainbow of oil on the surface of the water,
a spillage, an eruption

sliding over the moon-hauled tides
and out into the constant depths off shore:

the constant future

where suspended underneath the waves
inside the deep green silence

a seagull's wing beat,
or a motor's hum

or the thud of the container's hull
moored up tight against the harbour wall,

wait for their return at the end of the tide.

And that water is my own.
I also live inside it.

O hear me call
in the flux of sunlight.

I am not the dryness in the shadows.
I am not a cloudless sky.

I made this song from the river,
sculpted it from wave and driftwood.

O I am abundant and you are not.
Howl to the sea. Howl to the salt.

High Tide

A lyric for Emily Portman

Sail me, city, to heavens below.
Sail me, city, into depths of dark.
Sail me, city, into the hook of the estuary.
Sail me, city, to the clutch of the heart,

onto the high seas, under surfaces
through sunken shadow from old oil-lit shores
to the feline jaw of a tidal swish
and the bright-eyed bite of the cormorant.

I want the wild wet and the long depths,
strong undertow and tidal concerns,
but the harbour lights are drawing me in:
I fear dry land, sandbanks and stone.

Sail me, city, to heavens below,
Sail me, city, into depths of dark.
Sail me, city, into the hook of the estuary.
Sail me, city, to the clutch of the heart.

Onto the high sea, under surfaces
through sunken shadow from the old oil-lit shore
to the feline jaw of the tidal swish
and the bright-eyed bite of the cormorant.

O sail me, city, into the filth of the storm.
Bring the salt from my pores; let my eyes colour dawn.
O city, sail me away from settled land
into ocean's wreck and rough; back into love.

Please do not leave me earthbound.
Please do not leave me earthbound.

The Channelling

A boy in the woods stands still,
   grows old
   in the heat
   of an incoming storm,
  wakes, younger, skin soft,
    cries as his body returns to seed
     and pools on the earth,
     a dew swept into the wind,
     a swarm of bees.
He forms a woman,
   hair a red sunset,
  walks as her across the moss,
   sings a bright word
  which sounds like the wind
    as darkness streams towards the forest.
He thins into the soil, rolls
  like a dog,
   rots,
   feathers become owl
  and through the tops
   of the dark-wood-leaf
      night-sodden-eyes
    see only slips in light,
  the shadows between shadows,
    talons reaching out like splintered wood
     claw a vole in the leaf-mulch,
    a drop of blood on the frond
  as he seeps into the root,
    dissolving into the rain like paper.
His pulse finds a bloom to dwell in,

falling back into the night, pollen
        flung across the tree-stump by a sharp breeze –
he slows and breathes
        laid out across the rotten bark. Darkness
                comes again
                        and again.
The stream swells
        over his upturned face.
                Water
calls him back
        into the whole of itself,
forms a man swimming out to sea –
        diving into the flow,
        not needing to breathe,
for the air is also water
which smothers the trees,
his long hair sticky
        with the wet of the sun's
simmering voice. A woman
        floats by on the tide like a koi,
flicks her wet hair
        and walks inland,
        leaves a trail
of shimmering gold
        across the path like a snail.
She shakes herself down, lies still.
He strokes her thighs, blinks and watches the sky weld to
sound.
        A spark.
                Dawn is stretching its neck as the tide

lengthens and flattens
out beneath in a
a rich upturned blue.
She ties his hair to the trees like an anchor.
He is the blue juice of thunder,
a violet sunrise,
a full flush of rain.
He swims under the tide
as it curls
into him
made of flow,
of blood,
one state to another.
He walks amongst the trees,
bucolic, unburnished eyes
steaming up as the leaves burst into green.
The sun loops over the branches.
His heart is beating into his bones
as he thins,
is a woodland hare or deer,
an electric shock.
He stalks the sun,
body lithe, unbroken.
Pale chest cool and clean as the light.

Bridie's Tomb

August 2016, St James Cemetery, Liverpool

The pall-bearers balance on the wet grass,
finding their footing as the coffin
is carried along the slope towards the well.
The only well in Liverpool which can heal the dead,
I've heard it said by the dead
who laugh and giggle behind the graves.

Sea-wind flings itself over the city
full-heartedly in a wide embrace.
Figures walk towards the mausoleum and then disappear.
Sun settles a little then runs into the cloud.
Children died. Five years. One. Gone.
The curl of the clock wrings the day dark.

'Hold still,' she says. 'Let me feel your pulse.'
I let her grab my wrist, thumb
my jugular, listen to the space
blood runs warm. Her eyes smile.
She sighs. 'Listen for us. The rough of
the walk; all hurt is hunger.'
A drum. Then a gull. Car on the road.

Stopping at the spring, the bearers
sip a drop and each sprout
wings from their shoulders. Feathered
white plumage, lift-on-up,
reheard as gulls squall on the salt.

'Be here,' she says. 'Be as sure as you can,
deep in the meld of your days.
Mine passed like waves, brocade
and parlours, distant view from the window
of the ships in the dock, unloading their
cargo. Father said not to look.
No. No-one said to see it all. We learnt
this after our house was
bought with the proceeds of others' pain.'

'How much of your life,' she says
turning to me white eyes alight,
'is balanced on the unseen,
scratched deep, long nights avoiding
sweats brought about by the shadows?
Or the bold extravagance of not caring,
of not being able. Are you able?'

She catches my arm, holds it up to the light.
A garnet ring shimmers in the afternoon sun.
'You are nearly undone. You hear us speak.'
I call out, 'Speak what?' 'Just listen,' she replies
'to what is out of sight, the closed room deals
and the casino nights. Listen to the men
as they make their pacts;
you might be part of an agreement, just like me.'

'He took me to the sea,' one girl says.
'I was sold to the night,' cries another
as she throws her arms around a tomb.
'I was whipped later. Never free.'
'I died of cholera, dysentery. No clean water.'

'Write what you hear, poet, or we will disappear.'

Anchorage

'All shall be well, and all manner of things shall be well.'
JULIAN OF NORWICH

This quiet is full of noises, children's voices,
a gull's rich cry, rattle of the electric heater, car
engine like a river in flood, my breath inwards
as the cold comes closer and now, now,
behind the wooden door poised to open it,
a woman in a wool beret with bobbed
black hair, curled at the ends, stands
palm on brass handle, her face turned towards
the children out-of-sight behind the pews,
outside the church, outside the cell,
running and laughing in a playground
of a school which isn't there, just new laid lawn:

on all sides the children are not there,
behind the door, coming closer,
behind the window, coming closer,
behind the stone, coming closer,

saying, 'Listen, we are outside the door
and as real as the window. We were here.
You missed us. We came but you didn't listen.
You didn't hear us when we spoke to you.
You only heard the distance.
Listen to the sound of others' silences,
of their absences, unsaid sighs and gut contractions.
In these moments we come to you and are seen
entering and not exiting; we are always in.
Always ask who else is there.

There will be many and they will want to speak
as the dusk speaks to shades of blue,
          rain-flowered and petalled with spring,
as the door speaks
                    in creaking deliberate opening,
as you speak in cautious glances,
as silence blows like last night's gale
                    out of the window and away,
as the world moves around us and us into it,
no out-there but always here,
as we curl towards each other to see ourselves appear.'

St James's at Dusk

Today the light is as faded as the sound
of the street above the cemetery.
A crow caws on its flight above our heads,
over the weight of bodies leaning into the dusk
until all of us are sinking in the rush of the afternoon.
A couple seen at the bus-stop, fresh from the train,
walk past again holding hands – we are still to meet.
And somewhere in the mush
freshly wrought beginnings rustle in their sleep,
dust off the damp of their winter coats, shake
plumes of curly hair and flushed cheeks,
walk along the track back up towards the mausoleum,
sandstone glowing gold as the sun sets
over the Welsh mountains'
burning snowy tops, light spooling out and across
the rocks which spin the red heat
like the hands of a clock.

St James's at 3 a.m.

Car tyres catch on ice-crusted tarmac,
    a taxi turns right along Hope Street
        as a young woman with black-lined eyes stares
            hard out of the glass. He sees her look
            for him,
            look for nothing,
            down and down
                into the city's empty vein.
        He is a body laid out amongst the bushes,
            heart-rate slowing, sleep approaching
            as a vibrant blue-sheened freeze
        cups around tombstones
    in the thrust of night as it sweeps,
        low and wild,
    across the hollow below bare trees
        and into the fallow dark.
And he lies in his shelter
    under a tarpaulin stretched round thin trunks
        on the slope on the rise,
    between the dead and the drunks
        in steamed-up pubs along cobbled side-streets;
            and deep below in pure dark,
                graves are as silent as the sea,
        some rustle, some murmur,
            but he cannot hear muffled
        in a sleeping bag, nose touching crystalline air.
His eyes see car headlights flit
        over leaves like insects
    as he turns his back, old shoulders
        pressed into solid ground, stones

            nibbling into his skin
        and he remembers everything,
        faces and movements,
                the crack of the light.
And the dead, he tells himself, can't hurt him:
        they are the long-gone past, a past
                turned over and mulched down in the rot.
He carries the living past like a rope
        which twines its grasp around his breath
        out here in the scratching cold
        as we, a murder of crows,
                    perched atop the catacombs
            angling for action,
                    peck out the shadows,

strip back the stains from the street-lamps,
and light a red bonfire by the sacred well.

St James's in December

At Bridget's well a boy presses a girl
into the wall, their winter coats khaki green
against the redbrick, his hand on her waist,
her blonde hair scraped back
as they start to fall and slide,

water leaching into their trainers,
weed on crisp air, two bulldogs
in piles of leaves where the gravestones end.

And the slip of it is a weight
that drags you under, a ship's ballast
as you drown, light nods to dark,
a background flit of starlings,
white-froth-breath submerged
in the quarry before the graves,

down to the stone cut and deciphered
into blocks to build a church, a hall, a court.
Grey horses pull loads up the ceremonial route.

And as the couple kiss, wet tongues
at the edge of teeth,

teeth in the graves clatter,
splutter through soil for a second,
eyes open in the dark
know nothing but the quiet,
lung of rot and an empty skull;
one gull like a siren,

a fog on the coast
as your ship sinks down
and under into the frost.

St James's in August

This is where all the tears are. They run underneath the rock
and through the graves. In the muddy ground liquids
merge to form a body walking slow, unclothed across the flags.
He smiles, seems familiar, has a look of someone going home.
He walks among the trees, touching the trunks.
Each bark shivers, shifts to skin, becoming everything,
becoming nothing. And when the ship left him at the harbour
he climbed across the rigging, unseen but determined,
running away from his father and now he is leaving
and will not say goodbye. He will not say anything
to the clouds, river, sky. In the graveyard he walks
like a stag as the trees fall down as the light is felled
by his movement, coursing through the bloodlines of the cemetery,
though no body rises and he stands still
looking into the eyes of the trees as they sway,
then, as always, hurrying and moving on in full flood
down the arteries that pump life back into the stone
as it flows, he goes, grabs the rain and wears it like a cloak.

Passage Grave

Inside the chamber each pattern is alight
as a strip of sun seeks damp shadow
within chiselled grooves to swirl the bright into black.

The light, deep inside the dark,
finds new routes across the rock.
Each grain of sandstone is compressed time,
a salty fleck in a watery suspension,

moving within and across the solid matter
to restart and renew its shift into shadow.
The shadow becomes lit and the light
becomes dark.

The stone is not inert
but processing the darkness, turning it back into
light, light turning back into dark,

as years spiral onwards and into the rain,
prescient on the horizon,

grey cloud about to burst with this moment
woven and weaving one day to the next.

Song Cycle

Imbolc

I want to stay in the weather,
within the feel of the rain,
within the soft call of the wind,
within the light on the sand.

I want to stay in the weather,
inside the curve of the sky and call of the birds.
I want to stay in the weather,
inside the whole of the light,
inside the touch of the day.

I am a fall of leaves,
a crisp under-foot layer of mulched-down matter.
To turn into the city is to turn to brick.
How heavy that is.
How hard to shift.

BELTANE

I am the flow of your blood
and the touch of the moon.
I am your love boiling over on a summer's day.
I am your heart burnt by too much sunlight.
I am your laughter crumbling into the long grass.

O little lover –
you are my heart and the flower of me.
I pitch out into the May Day air.
I am at the centre of it all as I fall
into you, bloom, and back into stars
and sweat. I am at the centre of it all –
sad-faced on an empty street
or in the moon-lit park
or in the alley that leads to the bridge.

Let me go. Let the heat go south for the winter.
Am I not here? I am everywhere
and you are within me, every stroke of my hair,
eyelash blink, flat-line of your eye.
I am everywhere and O I am not.

LUGHNASADH

Under the trees light is a tissue,
layers stuck to layers, light upon light.
I peel it back slowly to see what hides
long and wet in the deep shadow,
flattened out and moulding in the summer air.

A stare – an eye looks back up from the mud.
One large green baleful eye blinks, closes,
opens like a cloud passing away from the sun.
I use my fingers to remove the earth.
From the rest of the head a nose protrudes,
a mouth opens, breath like a gale
pulling me into the swell of the shadow.

I cannot see the sunlight, the trees
lean in and cover me with their branches
like a swaddled child. Here in the glade
behind the old oaks the head shakes
grains of soil from its skin,
seems to settle, keeps staring
up at the sky, caught behind the green,
long eyelashes like new shoots
flicker in the spray of soil flung
from my hands' rough digging, scraping
at the edges to carve out a space to see.

There is no body, just this face in the mulch
watching the trees grow, watching time pass.

I have to keep the vision clear.

When the snow comes I melt the frost.
When the dry winds crack the mud
I scrape away the dust.
When the leaves fall I shift the slurry
with these hands. I see the changes
that time cannot. I need eyes to mark
the distance beyond these gnarly trunks.

A fox runs in the long grass.
I hear him howl. He catches the sun in his tail.

He meant to catch the moon.

Now he runs away with the stars
which are not the only light in his eyes –
burning orange fur, a fire screeching
across the landscape like a comet.

SAMHAIN

When the dark came
I was sleeping. He knocked at the door
in the middle of the night.
I let him in while dreaming.
He saw all my fear, all my fright
cornered like a lamplit hare.
Shivering, he was a green man
and I was a ghost.
The night walked across the threshold
and the seed was laid
beneath the corridor, roots like algal bloom
swelled in the air and carried me to you-

O love you are a river.
I am full of silt.
I want the world to ache,
to feel this throbbing
as the evening falls, exhausted,
across the woodland floor.

My love is like a footstep
quiet on the earth, unheard
until I wake you from
shelter in the dry lands
beyond the restive tide.

I pour my hurt upon you
across all space and time.

The ghosts, they sing –
I hear them in the leaves.

They sing from behind my eyes,
from flesh, from out of me.

Green Lane

He walks from the monastery after a long night.
The light is a soaken-blue, his coat is wet.
The rain pours over his eyelids. Old oaks
line the way. He hums to himself, fretful in the grey
as the moon sinks over the cloud-tops like a cat.
He must find his way through the gloom
as head-on-pillows-empty-spaced-dreams
flow spare out of the windows.
He catches them in his hat like tiny birds.
A light in the convent taps on.
A woman sings a long note out into the night.
He bats it back. She catches it and sighs
as the grandfather clock ticks
its tune across the empty corridor of the old house,
a shadow-fuelled, tile-floored well of dark
where time waits to be let out into the blue-black,
singing 'I am here, I am here,' but nobody hears
as they sleep in their duveted beds,
rustled-up-comfy against the long-necked call of dawn.

Allerton Oak

At night, you grow taller. Branches rise,
now no longer one trunk split to three
but one unbroken pulse of green
up towards the cloudless sky
and the windows of the mansion house
where a woman stands at a turret window
as the building gilds itself with gold
and it is morning for her and work to be done
as she carries a brass scuttle, apron on,
down to the fire in the high-ceilinged hall,
shaking with the chill of dawn;
black dust in the fingerprint of her thumb,
as she kneels to sweep embers with a wooden brush,
piles kindling on the grate, then coal
from the old wood dug from the hillside
by miners deep beneath the heather,
one weak beam from an old oak above
supporting the heave of the mountain's ache.

The Lighthouse

A red buoy in the straits
and a bell at intervals.
Waves in thrall to the wind
lilt and roll. Rock-pools
hold handfuls of water,
pebbles under the still
salty sheen seem to
shine, so the sea says,
shifting and lolling,
reeling and following
the fold of the white waves
over the teal green
seagull bobbing modulations –
a light sun spattered
with rainwater. At the whole
of it, wet stone covered with
green algae. The bell again.
What if the movement isn't progress?
Time pulls differently
in the sea, falls to the sides,
falls away into flows
of algae eaten by seals
and fish caught by birds.
Endings come at different
tides, not at once,
not at the same moment,
not after and before,
but within the swell of the bell
chiming at intervals
which do not exist.

Second Self

You walk late
and loaded with landscape;
a basket on your shoulder.

You reach over the gate
and pull at my coat.
Fabric scratches, cuts and folds.

Flurry of hail against a shaken window.
You wonder.
You fold. You bend.

You wait in the street.
We are always in the street,
in the loneliness, in the potential

that never reaches over.
Can you not see me on
the other side?

You look and see only the path,
windows and wall, redbrick,
the painted door.

You hear a voice in your head,
books on shelves,
a computer screen on,

shoes on the floor
but no women there,
no one at all.

You do not expect to
ever see me. There are your things.
You left your key at work.

The dusk is crumbling over
the suburbs. It loves you
as it carries the dark.

When it comes you are
smothered, a shimmer in the eve,
a reflection in the window – looking for me

in the fold of the dusk
which carries you on,
back along the path,

one step over the flags
and the weeds to the corner by
the nursery, its lights

turned on by an early arriver,
black trousers newly ironed,
mascara drying in the radiated air.

And you will turn, just as dawn
bounces over the railway bridge
like a lost hare

and you will look both ways
and walk home again
tired, bleary eyed;

your walk from work
a slippery trail which shimmers
like an opened vein

and here you are again
the last leg back
to the front door to the gate

where I wait for you
holding out a hand
you can not see

as you cross over my waiting hold
to rebound again into the world.

The Bones' Lament

O the lovely slicing of the cold
and down into the wet,
down into the emptiness,
a thinning seam of depth.
My knee joints lie like stars
flung out across the bay.
From above I am a map,
a route to guide the way.
'Why drag me back together?'
I whisper to the moon.
'I like being multiple
down here inside the gloom.'
How to leave this watery bed?
I like being calcified.
I like the light as it filters in
and out of the turning tide.
And I like that I'm a tale told
in pubs at closing time.
Why do you need to know
exactly who I am?
What else do you want of me
up there upon the land?

The Burning Man

on the hill stretched out on a rack facing the view,

his white skin on fire singeing at the edges
like paper. He has fluffy brown hair.

It also singes. He is looking out at the city
with his head held high.

He is warning. He is a beacon on the hill.
He can be seen for miles, an apparition.

A warning. A warning.

I view him from behind as I walk down the path.
I cannot see his face, just his naked back.

The parkland grass is freshly mown and wet.
Dusk is coming. And he is burning.

Who set him on fire?
Who asked for him to burn?

He is a Christ-gone-wrong; threads of an age

but he can be seen for miles
and he does not scream or cry.

A warning. A warning.

Man is on fire
and we do not know what to do about the flames.

Space Time

Now, the wood unvisited must stand empty –

full of moon and darkness, the last trail of walkers:
a small fire burns ember-bright in the picnic ground.

This place has fences which line the site.

I lean on these, back in time,
tired by the giddying distance
across the river back to my home and here.

No man *there. No* man *known or dreamed upon.*

But you I dream upon.

I wake next to your deep sleep.

You look at me with clear eyes
                as if you are from the future
                like leaves waiting for winter

blown in a spiral out across the city
                and all the other times
                        littering the light.

≈

The distance is dreamt.

Inside the space
between horizon and horizon
falls snow –

long drifts of it
pillowing down into the middle of the river.
Somewhere on this tide a tall ship appears,
rigs and mast astride a different wind.

The crew, hot on a summer's day.

The wind like a beak
pecks at the picture till it fades into snow again.

Time is cavernous and I get lost in him.

Spring Tide

In her death, my water-lily
bobs emollient with light,
buoyant on the ripples.
She has found new life.

Her breaststroke, a release.
Her costume made of scales.
Water on her face like hands
as the torrent takes her home.

The river ate her family,
consumed the ship with depth,
sunk her money and her health.
Now she swims inland.

The captain's cabin was a dark maroon,
cabinets a gnarly oak.

The light was dark
and the conversation cruel.

It was not her heart which broke.

The Ghost on the Stairs

She gazes out from the dusky light.
I see her face for a second in the shadow.
She weeps, holding the banister,
leaning into the darkness like an owl.

'If I was scared I wouldn't be able to speak,'
I say. It is like being seen by the sky.
'Each wall is a skin I have to fit within,'
she replies. 'The light is fading.'

She turns to the front door blown ajar
and walks towards its outline
painted white like a picture frame.
And when she steps on through

she glances round to look at me.
She has my eyes, my hair, my lips,
laughs at the moment my body fades
as the warmth of my skin shifts to grey.

And I am on the stairs carrying a scuttle,
watching for the rise of the step,
watching for the tip of the shadow,
watching for the master's fast hands

and she turns her back on me and walks
down the road and away into the city,
into its alleys and lanes which grasp
her and lead her freely into the arms

of a man who once slept with me
and into the home of a woman who
had my name, my coat, my keys
as I place my palms on the threshold

like pressing into a cold mirror
to see only the carriages and horses pass
and hear the master call for his pipe
and find myself, here, locked inside.

Moon Dark

Not today a loop of the same tide

but an unravelling,
a straddling,

a clutching of hands
looking out to the horizon across the valley

to where the clouds stream into the turbines
and are swung forwards

in a new formation,
cumulus-blooming.

I want a re-making, a new landing.

I call the moon from the day.
I call the ghosts from their hearths.

From all beginnings I call endings
and all endings I call beginnings.

I curl over your stories.

I want you to see me folding into the blinking night.

Huntress

The snow whitens, bright-red stained
fire cracks as I fix a kettle on the spit

and mark my plan
out on the ice with a chilled hand.

I have a route across the tundra.
I have a sense of this future

sketched with a stick
into the cracked earth.

I must go under.

Near the forest is an entrance
to a cave with a grid across its grin.

I must cut my way in
with the tools of my trade,

descend the rickety stairway.
There is no coming back.

The voice is only a whisper and I can't hear her.
She keeps saying –

'Come under, come under,
I have an offering for you here in the dark.'

A flame sparks up and I see myself staring back.
I pass myself a rock

born of lava flow,
encrusted with sharp splinters

which cuts my finger and as the blood drips

I disappear
like a poppy in winter,
like a crow flies towards a low sun,
like snow swept into a cave mouth,
like dust.

I hold the rock tight in my palm.
It throbs a heartbeat, red and raw

until this is all that I am –
a pulse swept along caverns like a winter's gale

curling through the old mine,
looking without eyes

for some bright thing
in the grey black,
        blue black,
        red black,
        bite.

I blow on into the dust
of the blast
of the shrapnel
of the seams of coal still visible.

I lick along the carbon,
tastes of salt and sweat

like a body at dawn
or of a self nearly far gone

down into the deep stratum
which has nothing to reveal

just the pulse of her
bashing against the rock,

searching with scent
through the tiered levels

of the old mine workings,
tumbling, crumbling, remoulding

but how to climb out

and to be seen, to be known
by the people in the town –

to be said to be
and to be said,

to find you again amongst the smoke,
to hold a shape you recognise

for long enough to feel your pulse.

Memorial

Written on the occasion of the Black Chair Eisteddfod
Centenary Festival, Birkenhead Park 2017.

Rain erodes the old stone further and flows
    through rivulets of chiselled letters
        that name the past,
           who was here and who has died,
    the drops tumbling along the folds
        and over the ledge and over the railings,
mapping out the words in water –
        knowing again the moment of their incision,
           the fresh pain of the erection of the stone
when war was seared on everyone's vision,
        in dreams and in gestures,
in loss of sons and lovers, grief
        like a tidal inlet filling up again at dusk
like the pool that marks the headland
        at the birch trees where the priory stands
           as monks row their ferryboat
               out over the grey expanse,
        carrying travellers, pilgrims, soldiers
           away from their own present tense
               and to the other side.

But back in our town, straddling the edge of a determined river,
        to not be pulled away into the ocean
           is a feat of will.
The Mersey ferry pits itself
           against the tow; and the ship yards
    re-fit their hulls and keels
        as we all hold onto the land,

carving our names into the rock
> or the dead onto monuments,
> or our village in the mountains names the streets
> > migrants built after the journey
through grey-green valleys
> > > to a grey-green river
> and here sank new, less tangled roots
into the sandstone of our slippery shore.

We are embarkation and transformation,
> Paxton's utopia and Leverhulme's dream
of the pastoral masking dirt and rough cut
> hard grit of work of carving or building
> or withstanding no-work,
> > of days when the river
> could swallow us whole and our history
> > fell out-of-sight in the swell
to the darkest ebb of the ocean floor
> > which is salted like an untreated wound,
> > > blood poured into nothing to do,
> > > of not being held tight and left to drown –

always a sharp-edged town. From the windows in the big
houses on the hill
> we see ships dock in Liverpool
> > bringing cargo of sugar;

slavers unseen on the map that hangs on the school room wall.

And from the valleys, over the Dee come these memories,

comes the Welsh of Hedd Wyn and his song
in a language as ancient as the distance
to Birkenhead Park under the oak trees,
 and a two-tongued conversation of a town
which feels both of everywhere and of itself;
neither the city nor the village,
 half-mountain, half-redbrick terrace,
 half-salted ocean, half-freshwater;
and standing on the headland, under birch trees,
 the sun high as rain from Wales on the cumuli drifts inland
 and falls, cleansing the monument again,
 looping around the lettering,
we turn to see the dead walk inland
and cross the boundary to make ourselves a home.

City Farm

In the farmyard a pig lies in blood,
haemorrhaging again, in life on an edge
in the May heat, on straw and concrete,
fresh water in a bucket, flies in the roof-tress;
her body heaves and sighs answering to the moment,
which is a time, like these other times tapped out
into the day as the heat curls round her
shut eyes. She tries not to die.
The stable awning stretches like shoulders
and retracts unseen. Her arteries
flow with oxygen, sinews comfortable
as the guttering steadies under the weight
of sparrows sheltering from afternoon heat.

Along the path by the old chapel of rest,
on a headstone moss-inscribed dates moulder,
a curved shadow tips across the rise
by the gate-post and metal fencing.
Behind, in the deep green foliage –
nettles, elder, gorse – and in the mulch
insects sink beneath the sirens from the main-road.
Red roof tiles of the prison beyond,
ordered towards the sun,
still bright upon the afternoon,
border the old cemetery, stolid and squat,
as all the graves lean into the present,
tiring of gravity but still certain
of the cost of letting go.

And in the market garden, in the top soil,

spelt stretch their roots out slow,
long fingers burrowing into the dark
to capture nutrients, wetness, phosphorus
into their stalks and up in a steady push
towards the light; last year's crop bunched
into sheaves hanging in the eaves.
A kettle simmers in the office kitchen.
An email arrives in an inbox. A folder
of invoices in a binder balances
on the edge of a wooden desk. A cat
on the swivel chair, black and white fur steeped
in murky sun, stares out the four-paned window.

Night-visiting at Bridie's Well

I throw live ivy into the pool;
and nearer, water's load aplomb
falls straight onto gravel, lost
leaves submerged beneath wet cover

as Bridie sits beside me, a cotton slip
to the floor, damp at the hem,
fingers clasped at her lap, hair loose
as is she has just woken from sleep.

She looks ahead, doesn't turn her neck
but then is blown as a winter leaf
across the flags, tumbles as salted air
takes her like paper back to the graves

and behind the stone angel
a top-hatted man stands in grey like marble.
He is solidified winter.
He is watching me.

It is getting busier. They are gathering
like animals from the wood,
a stray gust and they all bend over
like the tips of the grass, whisper

our only sound is the water in the deep spring.
We move in how the small dog bounds,
turns his head to you, nods and is away

and Bridie blows through the cemetery,

seems to breathe but each deep breath
she holds as if she is diving under,
as if she may have drowned once

and has not let go of the air.
She reaches over me, a sea storm,
a cloud that opens and thunders down.
Blood my heart shared washes into the ocean

like twine into the mouth of seabirds.
They can't speak as they struggle,
stutter *Is there not enough air to breathe*
as unheard sound screeches across the city;

and the crowd among the catacombs
begin to sing a song beyond imagining.
I seem to hear them in the now night air
like the call of thunder. *Listen*, they say,

to the roll of silence in your eardrums.
We only speak as one,
a harmony of all our lives now gone.

We have become
sequences of notes in birdsong,
feet on mud across fresh shoots.

We call 'join us' but nobody does,
just an occasional sleeper
risen, like a wave, from their bed,

stepping in slippered feet
until the night returns to dawn
and you fly home towards the sun.

And we go on murmuring;
a blackbird perched high on branches
our nightly witness to the river:

and I, eyes wide open, look down.
I am that sleeper, dreamer,
now dusting across the eve
and I watch as far below

they are rain on an ocean
or fish at the surface risen for the heat.
They return to the cold,
to the cold that they are,

to the cold desire of the other side;
remember behind a wall, a door,
one full glance and you will hear
silence come visiting, bringing you a song.

Hearth-fire

In the other house,
sun has risen –
a reminder of light
and mountains across the straits.

In the other house,
a fire burns in the stove
and rooks circle
lines of trees

beyond the window, glass
opening the view into the room
where a wooden table
gleams in a streak of yellow.

In the other house,
starlings startle across a ridge,
a morning-rise of the future-tense,
up and outwards towards the sea

and all is opening
across the headland, hikers
stride and stretch
as the sheep run west

(In the other house,
a bed of knives welcomes
no-one – the house is
dark wood behind the fence.)

down their familiar tracks,
mud dried now, crust
upon wheel tracks
crisp under foot;

cloven hooves press into clay,
tap earth with their steps
away from seagulls
and their cry curling

across morning like a dream
of another house,
bound into the slope
with ivy and grass, a stone wall loop,

a wooden gate closed across a path.
In the other house,
sensing the dark as warmth,
the red grate seeps to embers

and a woman at a window
shuts a blind and I am
outside on the road
underneath night-fed sky.

Through trees two lights
form another shore
as the steep lane folds
like water around my feet

and I try to stand still
as in a boat at a jetty
watching fire in the stove
in the other house,

then I am over the hill again
down in the valley;
my hand rests on the stone cross
in shallows of sweeping dark

and I push into it as it
pushes back, taking my weight
into the centre of rock,
into grain and rough,

then pull back, palm flat,
skate a touch across film
then again full into the stone,
pulse in and out,

return to the road
which swirls beneath my feet
and the fire in this stove rages
as bright as sunlight,

gritty particles circle
between fingertips
like a fall of snow
cools into bone and I am lit.

The Ghost Talks to the Tree

Sometimes I hear you sing, often at dusk,
and you murmur like distant thunder rolls
then nothing more for days.
I sit and watch you from this tusk
of a landed tree, I fold
my non-legs into crosses and hold
nothing for you. No space. No light,
just the gap that is unfilled –
view straight through air to the park.

O bustle, O wing beat, O scold of sun
through crisp-edged branches,
pattern me, please, or I won't see
these hands within the daylight
or this hair twine into strands,
heat scaling out my absent body.

If I am not here, how do I hear?
I only hear with bodies laid
soft on the grass before the view
as if the view was an altar and they
the sacrifice.

Glisten for me green-winged dryad.
Fill this absence with extravagance,
with light and shade, with love
of emptiness, of the way back to before.
Tree – you curl and clip for me
though I am never here to let you know.

Skeleton Woman

Her bones begin to convulse,
a skeleton re-finding skin,

the juice, the mess, the light
as she walks into the day

looking for the sun, trying
to find the heat, but carrying

in her bag a great moon,
dirty, sooty, scraped with ash,

so heavy the bag cuts
her shoulder, knife-edged,

into the muscle; she is
an incision across her neck.

She drags the bag like a cart.
It rolls on tiny splinters,

scratches lines into the track
and sunlight moves on

like a wrecker's lantern
swung over foggy headland.

The way ahead is bound,
tied up with knots

and shadows and
in the bag are apples

becoming fetid
as sun catches their skin,

not hers, which is always
in shade under cloud.

Do the apples need to rot?
How do they decay?

Become a fleshy hand,
a skinful of blood.

They need more light,
a fierce heat, mouths

to eat them one-by-one:
teeth biting into flesh.

The Coach House

Distant berries on a thorn bush ripen
overnight as if taken by surprise
by the summer, pulse red bold bulbs
swollen with light and water against
the thick green-wet leaf: a relief
to see them appear. A man at a downstairs
window wonders, *late this year, so late.*
If I catch them at the moment they brighten,
I know I will live, am still alive.
To miss them is to die, he thinks, scratches the glass
with his nail. Dust squeals, is removed.
The view from his eye to the bush
is brilliant, spectral, scented
with the tang of blueberries, blackberries, red
falling to the floor like unread ink;
and in that moment they are gone
like cloud swum over the sky,
fish above a deep pool down onto
the unkempt path, a swallow swoop, a mallard's
dive, all creaturely descent across
the air, boiled nature shed to bone.
The man tightens the curtain, pulls
back into the dark, sits alone.

In Midsummer

A woman running through the shrubbery,
straight ahead through the rhododendron bush.
She has bare legs, a long shirt, bare feet,
runs as if the foliage isn't there,
running from something that follows her.
But there is nothing. No body comes.
Where is she going?
Here she is again. She turns, looks behind,
long blonde hair blown back.
For her it is night, I can see that –
and it has been raining. For me, it is heat
and a June-basked day in the glade
that works my sense – head to the left,
swift twitch to the right.
Here she comes again, on the same track
which isn't a track, a desire path
between conifers trips across her route.
She flits over wheatgrass, saplings
slimed with snail-drawn rivers.
What comes after her from the shade
between the silver birch? Beyond,
white of daisies on the lawn-green.
She runs from the right out of the sunlight,
appears – here she is again – from behind
the patina of holly leaves like woodblock
print against the sun. And then still in front of me,
her bare legs lean over where I sit on grass.
She turns her head, looks back,
looks forward, runs on, skims the purple
just-gone-over rhododendrons. I turn

to see her curve into the shadow
where leaf is bold and covers all
definition. And as my spine
twists on its pelvis, there she is again,
– who will break this? My
observation of her gesture keeps her looped
in the woodland glade forever. Where do I go?
How do I leave? A rustle in the trees,
blackbird hunting for grubs.

Costume in the Public Park

The dress, the shape of summers gone
when the days didn't weep or cry
but seemed to drift along
with no real end. The streets
rolled out like never ending rivers
swirling into the distance
full of sun and trains on the line
always going somewhere.
And I can't join this past:
the change needs to come quicker.
Nothing was lost as nothing was there.
Just a sandal, a curl of hair, straw hat,
croquet hoop markers
to plot the map back to here.
We try inside this to find a pattern
which sounds like ourselves
but really is the touch of all
the hands we've held, love made
on slow stormy days;
in the middle, just the wind –
a voile dress billowing forwards
empty, all the buttons undone.

Dialogue with Penmon Cross

I hear you. The light returns
through the small glass window
in the darkening dusk, in the quiet,
into my gut, a pull in my stomach
to coil into the shapes of your living,
carving, falling,
then out into the straits and the clouds.

I am drawn into the twine and I listen
for shifting movements
which tumble and are not me
– but are someone – longing
for the fold and skin,
to seep into the lengths of each
distance – far mountains, long grass,
reflections on water,
and to flatten out and shimmer there unseen.

The Well at Winter Solstice

Water sucks light slipt between trees,
moon opening out of the cloud
and under the cover of a slanted roof,
a flat black square edged with slate,
walls wet redbrick porous and sodden;
and across the lane, one-light-on,
a cottage at an angle to the earth
watches mountains across the straits,
car headlights scanning the seashore
like eyes reading ink; and he is here –
a foot on wet stone, marking the mass,
crushing life from lichen slipped down
into shallows, absorbed into darkness
that is his thighs, muscular legs rising
like a seal in the ocean after the hunt;
his skin drips with ink, the ink pool
stains grey moon-bit stone and he walks,
has a torso upon a lithe pelvis, steps
onto a ledge and bends low to be seen
by the shadow, held under the shadow
pressing onto his shoulders like a gale;
and in his nakedness, his night-lit watery cobalt,
he steps onto the grass and towards me
standing under the tree; he does not see me
for I am wall and bark and stone and moss:
I see with their eyes as he treads
heavy blue-black onto winter-cut grass
and gravel rolls under each step, sharp
clicks to smooth and the tree branch tip
flicks with a change in air-pressure,

as the stream eyes him like an eclipse
high above its flow, his liquid hair at his waist;
he wades across crushed stones,
and down through me, unseen, in his way.
I close my eyes and the night is blank,
my mind submerged in pigmented depth.
I fall out of this temporary self,
his tune in my mouth wet and warm
forms long notes of an ancient song,
a chant I do not know. My lips taste salt,
and his voice is deep ground,
sung like cattle low across empty fields
and a rustle in the openness
as he reveals the graves, the church beyond
which is listening and the stone cross
behind the screen in the dark
startles and hears me, hears us sing
out across the sea; the patterns re-ravel,
the water in my voice swollen
with the lick of his steps, heavy, certain,
down the signposted track to the car park,
past the hut and the sleeping cat,
past the barred gate and the cows in their barn,
past the twine, tyres, feed,
plastic wrap, new laid posts
and into the quarry and into the sea
and under the sea into the tide
and into the tide, into the cave
at the ocean bed where mountains
root like teeth into soft sand

and into the end of the light
where no moon slips within
and no words are heard or visions seen.
In the cave, I swim in him and him in me
and we come to be like we began,
silence speaking as loudly as he can.
Listen: he talks of a river with a rocky shore
and a woman bobbing in the water,
her face smiles to the sky, dreams
of long beaches, sea creatures
and sunsets over the sea-salty estuary,
of the far ocean and the deep return
as we crawl ashore on hands and knees,
our skin on sharp sand grazed pink,
sticky grit, cold tight on bare backs,
to where shingle turns to bramble –
standing at last, naked, walking steady
through the quarry and through the farm
towards the cottage and the light,
towards the stream and freshwater,
towards the well at winter solstice,
along the path towards the pond
under the gateway built of limestone,
where he leans now on the far side
in shadow, his hair blows like ivy blows
as if he doesn't have to travel anywhere today
but will rest and watch the blue sky turn grey
and the light slide away into the year,
watch as I pace up new-laid path
pulling shrivelled blackberries from the bush;

then I am there at night, shaken in the dark,
then there at dawn, cold in reluctant light,
then there or next year, another solstice,
my steps, sticky slow on a summer's day
or a sodden run through fresh fallen rain.
Still the spring stream disappears, unseen
into folds of leathery green, as snow
arrives out of the distance, sun
burrows into many horizons,
rays like bells ringing out of the soil.
And then stillness at the well but weighted
down, not a swim in deep water
but a shallow dive through to find
the basin bottom where copper pennies
lie like wreckage or many fallen suns.
I lower myself into the cold, squat,
avoid sharp stones on my soles,
and my body collapses like the skin it is;
all bone and blood pools into the well.
I am fluted, folded over like a cloth.
And in the rectangle of the entrance, framed
walking up the path, he has been to the shore,
trails seaweed behind each step like tentacles,
puts his hand into water, into me,
swirls the pool like wind in a tree.
Within the flow, feel how the spring,
so slow circles, churns over in a spin.
I am a sea-otter coiling somersaults
as he washes fresh salt into this bath of me,
turns and lies on wet grass like a tired dog

and from across the coast, dense sea fog,
a diesel engine hiss stills at a distant jetty;
one slant of thin sun slips into the mud.
There is no speech here pushing through;
the clear liquid now puddled with me
becomes inkier, loaded with deposits,
like a rock turning over in the tides
left to soak in flows from beyond my grasp:
an owl balanced on the branch, shut-eyed;
a rat in dark rivulets scurries through.
A bat overhead curves back as dusk
sinks again; always the day is lost
as I wash away one inscription
and listen for the next. And when
my body reappears as snow, as raven,
as tree, as fish, as hillside, as reflection on the pond,
as reed bed cut low for winter,
as pine needles on a gravel path,
as sun over the horizon from the next day,
as sea-wind miles inland softens the skin,
I pull myself up out of the water,
shake her down, dry her in the wind.
Sharp sky picks through the distance,
starlings rise at speed above my head.
Heart-beat, breath, gull-cry, rain-soon
sounds in my skin, mud catches toes.
He stands and drips sea-salt, all light,
down into the well, dampness glows.
A voice calls my name. I know the sound.
A light in the cottage beats on, then off.

And I look out from the kitchen window
at mountains framed by white flaking paint;
behind, two children at a low table,
faces caught in the hands of the moon.
They just sit static, painted-on,
and the night stares hard, watches
to see how I move towards them
as if they are real children. Outside,
a man and a women shuttle along,
seem to be sodden, seen to be caught in the rain,
but there is no rain, just the reign of the moon
and a man standing at an open door.
He arrives in a raincoat every evening
but he has only been to the shore
from where he drops a tide of pebbles
on the threshold and shakes silt
out from his hair; as the door closes
he becomes the raincloud that he is
and all I see through the streaky pane
is his face shift from man into wave,
pour like a waterfall over the gorse.
And the rain on the roof is my relation,
also dripping down inside the well,
and he comes again over the ocean,
in from the cave in the shape of a storm
as the brickwork turns its inside to the wind,
and outside I turn and the cottage
is stone-dark-blue, no one-light-on,
just tree-shadowed curve to the fence,
and he is sat on a wall on the headland,

back-turned, and he is stood at my side
as if he is my shadow long laid into dark.
The sea slops at the jetty over the rise
as we travel along the stony path,
towards the empty well where he bends
all swollen whole of his liquid self,
dives head first back into the basin,
and I smooth into sleet and high wind
across open sea, all the flush of me
in a strong hold, pushing my spine,
bending my back over into a wave,
speaking into my ears with a cold that pierces,
for my eyes to look through to see the way,
for this mouth to call out to gravity and all force,
for my hands to snap and break to fling,
to take part in the erosion and I am willing,
I can hear it asking in each gesture,
pummelling of pressure; and I cup my hand
and drink him in, my tongue and gullet
flushed with liquid scooped from the well.
Water shines through my bones like glass,
like a sun through cloud it streams
between my legs, out from my mouth,
from my hair which is also water,
rivers of it, waves splash across a forehead
of rain clouds and midwinter mist,
a haze of sea-salted air blooms and blows
as my belly and eyes flood and gush,
palms dip to hold then still again;
and strewn across the winter grass,

over the well-stream which runs to the sea
and into the woods, downy feathers;
and in the undergrowth, a pigeon
red-belly and taloned legs facing the sky.
All the coins have been taken from the well.
A stray penny lies on the wet stone.
In an alcove, two twigs bound with dried grass
and a red candle burnt down low.

Keeping the Doors Open

'Why should the modern displace the ancient,
around which cluster so many sacred associations?'
      REV. W.D. WOOD REES, *A History of Barmby Moor*, 1911

Light on a bay roof, slither of sun across a lawn,
a mammoth's tooth on the leather-lined table,
dust on a pile of papers by the window, beyond
a garden, camellia crisp with ice
and row of fir trees line a mossy sandstone wall;
black wrought-iron gate open to the road
and across the country lane a redbrick boundary
and then the parish church of Barmby Moor,
stained-glass window high above the cemetery
where a figure stands, white collar at his throat,
a long wool cassock to the uncut grass,
and he waves with one hand towards the porch,
walking ahead of me one step at a time.
He turns inside, under the carved wood mantle
and pauses at the doorway, as I do.
Inside is a different church, back in Llanrhidian,
January sun seeps through dimpled glass
as at the altar stands another man in vestments
who holds high a chalice, passing communion
to parishioners, kneeling, invisibly, at the step.
Behind me, in the porch, a lamp catches on,
a lamp no-longer there, shines as if lit for the first time
and a quick woman's voice and three men talk
beyond the walls. Their footsteps tap away
along the path and I look towards the altar
and the priest is walking down the aisle, inscrutable,

an eye to a hand held out from the front row,
and as he reaches the space in front of my breath,
this cold inwards air, he thins, disperses; in one gulp
I draw him in, breathing my self back into the light.
A knock at the door of the closed porch. The light is off,
the light has gone. I walk in from a bright summer's day,
stay still, can't move, locked in the transition,
then disintegrate, coil, find myself, finger-in-the-soil,
curling back ivy for a name carved on long-eroded stone,
grit of dried earth under my nails, a moment
inside the grave, laid quiet in the still of the coffin,
then wormed through the body of a yew
whose trunk sinks into my torso like a last breath,
then flat and thinned, long and lean, crawling
along its branches, an ear to the estuary in the distance;
a drum sounds from the limestone outcrop below,
and the church is a cliff-face and the marsh is a sea
and the beat throbs; and songs are sung later
in the church hall; – comic, music-hall, a ballad –
notes turned to one register I reach into and I am gone.

Resonances: An Afterword
by ROSI BRAIDOTTI

Do not let the emotional impact of Eleanor Rees' poetry mislead you: there's intense intellectual rigour at work here, as well. This collection pursues a consistent hypothesis, supported by razor-sharp intuitions. And it builds them up into a sequential, clear vision. It is moving on the affective level, but also knowledgeable and conceptually stirring.

Rees' poems go a step beyond neo-materialism, though they manifestly belong to this philosophical tradition. What the readers will find here is an elemental, lyrical quality that gets to the core of living matter. All that lives, lives in constant flow, fully lost and fully formed at the same time, always in process. What we call matter is like weather – forever changing, unfolding and rebounding. Living matter expresses a potential that never reaches over completely, but never ceases to strive, as if yearning for an endless future. Time and space do not separate and divide, but rather swell in and through a continuum of endings and beginnings. They live on, in and through me, but mostly out of me.

This is poetry that reads you back to yourself: both reflexive and reflective. It approaches the intensities of life, engages ethically with their force and invites you to take them on. Will you ever know how much a body can take? At heart, *The Well at Winter Solstice* sings out, and experiments with, the cognitive powers of poetry.

The poems are light of touch, but ponderous in thought. They argue over and over again that all entities are nomadically everywhere, and not fixed substances with solid boundaries. Even I am everywhere and yet I am not. I am just passing through, though I have a strong, distinct sense of the future, of what may yet come to be the case, even after I am gone.

Eleanor Rees produces a poetic treatise on the trans-corporeal, eco-sophical nature of what we unthinkingly call Life. Life is not one metaphysical unit, but rather a complex singularity of heterogeneous instances. It is matter as meta-morphically alive, flowing across all sort of constituted entities. These poems draw out the infinite beauty of living matter and of enduring time, honouring their stubborn and at times disconcerting vitality. All the while they enact a subtle indifference to anthropocentric self-importance. For thinking, feeling and understanding – pain and hope – are the stuff of the world, not the prerogative of any humans.

In Rees' work, planetary and cosmic forces are distilled with the precision of a master chiseller, framed by the rhythms of a classical ballad. Patterns of lovingly wrought repetitions point to the ancestral memories of things past, but never quite gone. Proceed with caution, as if taken by surprise. Not all movement is progress, so move gently, if move you must.

These poems are written in a state of grace, trusting in the infinite wisdom of the universe. And Rees gives us hope that all manner of things shall be well in the end, if we are able to shift our vision. She encourages us to cultivate the desire to become imperceptible, to learn to listen to what is still out of sight, but only for here and now. Because much of our life, as it multiplies and tumbles along, is balanced on the unseen.

Acknowledgements

'Queenfisher' in *Abridged 0–29: Primal*, Derry, June 5, 2013; 'Saltwater' in *Burial Of Sight*, Word Hoard, 2012 and also commissioned for and performed at Radical Liverpool, a Happening on Hope Street, Everyman Theatre, 2011; 'High Tide' a lyric for folk singer Emily Portman performed on *Coracle*, Furrow Records, 2015; 'High Tide' also in *Riverine*, Gatehouse Press, Norwich, 2015; 'Dialogue with Penmon Cross', *Sandspout Magazine*, Albion Beatnik Press, Oxford, January, 2017; an earlier version of 'Bridie's Tomb', 'Women on Brexit', *Poem*, London, June, 2017; 'St James's at 3 a.m.' commissioned for 'Tonight at Noon, a celebration of fifty years of The Mersey Sound', Bluecoat Arts Centre, 20th June, 2017; 'St James at Dusk' in *Poetry Ireland Review* 124 Autumn 2017; 'Memorial' published in the anthology of The Black Chair Eisteddfod Centenary Festival, Birkenhead Park, 2017; 'Moon Dark' in *Smoke* 60; 'In Midsummer' and 'The Lighthouse' in *Abridged 0–53: Relapse*, Derry, 2018; 'St Seiriol's Well' in *Poetry Wales,* Bridgend, Autumn, 2018.

With thanks for generative conversation and inspiration to: Silvia Battista, Desdemona McCannon, Judy Mazonowitcz, Lizzie Nunnery, Emily Portman and Steven Shakespeare. Thanks to Dave Ward for editing, support and imagination. Thanks also to the Gommon family for use of Ty Joseff. Thanks to Liverpool Hope University.

With thanks to The Northern Writers' Award 2018, New Writing North and Arts Council England.

A special thank you to Professor Rosi Braidotti, Utrecht University, for her generous afterword.

Notes on the Locations

St James Garden is a Victorian cemetery below Liverpool Anglican Cathedral. Originally a quarry, it is estimated there are 57,774 burials. Closed in 1936 the cemetery is now a public park. At the centre on the north wall is St Bridget's Well. A natural spring, it flows into a manmade basin and is said to predate the quarry and the cemetery.

St Seiriol's Well is located at Penmon Priory on Ynys Môn (Anglesey). A hermitage site from the 6th century, St Seiriol was said to be Seiriol the Fair as he walked across the island with the sun behind him. An 18th century hut covers the holy well, while outside the wild spring flows down towards the sea.

Llanrhidian is a village on Gower Peninsula, South Wales. Rev. George Edgar Rees was vicar there 1850–1896 and is buried underneath the yew tree. Barmby Moor is a village near Pocklington, Yorkshire, England. His son, Rev. William Wood Rees was vicar there, 1885–1932.

NEW POETRY FROM SALT

DAVID BRIGGS
Cracked Skull Cinema (978-1-78463-207-6)

MICHAEL BROWN
Where Grown Men Go (978-1-78463-208-3)

PETER DANIELS
My Tin Watermelon (978-1-78463-209-0)

MATTHEW HAIGH
Death Magazine (978-1-78463-206-9)

ANDREW MCDONNELL
The Somnambulist Cookbook (978-1-78463-199-4)

ELEANOR REES
The Well at Winter Solstice (978-1-78463-184-0)

TONY WILLIAMS
Hawthorn City (978-1-78463-212-0)